MICHELLE OBAMA

OBAMA

MEET THE FIRST LADY

MICHELLE OBAMA

OBAMA

MEET THE FIRST LADY

by David Bergen Brophy

Collins

An Imprint of HarperCollins*Publishers*

Collins is an imprint of HarperCollins Publishers.

Michelle Obama: Meet the First Lady
Copyright © 2009 by David Bergen Brophy

Library of Congress Cataloging-in-Publication Data is available.
ISBN 978-0-06-177991-6 (trade bdg.) — ISBN 978-0-06-177990-9 (pbk.)

1 2 3 4 5 6 7 8 9 10
❖
First Edition

For my parents

Contents

MICHELLE OBAMA

OBAMA

MEET THE FIRST LADY

Prologue

The thunderous applause rose to a deafening crescendo in the Pepsi Center stadium on a warm August night in Denver. Then, the cheering slowly died down as a tall, forty-four-year-old African-American woman took her place at the podium and began her speech at the Democratic National Convention. As the 4,500 people in attendance listened along with millions of prime-time television watchers at home, the woman who would be the first African-American First Lady in U.S. history began to tell her story. "Each of us," Michelle LaVaughn Robinson Obama said, "comes here tonight by way of our own improbable journey."

This is the story of Michelle Obama's journey.

1 Hometown: Chicago

"Hog Butcher for the World,
Tool Maker, Stacker of Wheat,
Player with Railroads and the Nation's Freight Handler;
Stormy, husky, brawling,
City of the Big Shoulders."

In 1916 the great American poet Carl Sandburg called Chicago the "city of the Big Shoulders" in his famous poem. He meant that the city was a busy, hardworking place just like the busy, hardworking people who lived there. Starting in the early 1800s, settlers of all kinds pushed into the vast area of America known as the West in their relentless search for more land and opportunity for themselves and their families. Chicago's geographic location put it at the heart of this western migration.

Chicago, with its deepwater seaport on Lake Michigan, was in the perfect position to serve as the center for growing trade with the rest of the emerging nation. Farmers who harvested their grain and stockmen who raised livestock all looked to Chicago to process and ship their produce, by rail and by ship, to hungry cities in the East.

During the last one hundred years, even as markets have changed and transportation methods have evolved, Chicago has remained a lively, competitive place to work and live. While rail traffic has slowed, O'Hare International is one of the busiest airports in the United States. Although the slaughterhouses that once covered the back lots of the city are gone, towering skyscrapers of international trade and commerce companies have taken their place. This is the city that Michelle LaVaughn Robinson Obama was born into and remains a citizen of today.

"I am the product of a working-class background," Michelle Obama said with pride to audiences all over America when giving speeches in support of her husband's historic run for president. "I saw hard work and sacrifice every day." Specifically, the little girl from the South Side had her own father to look to as an example. She was proud that her father, who was employed by the Chicago municipal water department, "[had been] a city worker all his life."

Decades earlier, Michelle's father's father and millions of other African Americans had been a part of a great change that the city of Chicago had undergone.

At the end of the Civil War in 1865, when slavery was abolished, the economy of the United States was dependent mostly on small farmers and local skilled workers. Several generations after the end of the Civil War, the economy of the country became industrialized. As jobs became scarce in rural areas, work opportunities shifted to the cities.

The cities were growing, and jobs in factories, railroads, stockyards, and other businesses were plentiful. All of these industries needed workers. For years, these jobs had been eagerly filled by the Irish, Poles, Lithuanians, Germans, Italians, and other European immigrants who had sought better prospects than their native lands offered. But when World War I began in 1914, this flow of immigration began to slow down and native-born Americans, many from the South, began to take the immigrants' places in industry.

The move away from rural, agricultural areas would become known as the Great Migration. This huge relocation of families would take place over several generations. Millions of people, primarily blacks, would leave their homes in states like Alabama,

Mississippi, and North and South Carolina. They would settle with their families in the growing northern cities. This migration would change the face of urban America forever.

Chicago was such a city, and it became the destination of more than half a million African Americans from the South. Originally comprising just 2 percent of the city, by the year 2000, blacks would make up more than one-third of Chicago's population. One of them was Fraser Robinson, Jr., Michelle's grandfather. He was a descendant of slaves. A brickmaker by trade, the elder Mr. Robinson left Georgetown, South Carolina, and settled on the South Side of Chicago.

2 Growing Up

Michelle's father, Fraser Robinson III, spent his whole life working for the Chicago water department. In his early days he was a common laborer expected to do such manual tasks as cleaning, mopping, and performing general janitorial detail. Later, when he had more experience and years on the job, his work became more administrative and less physically demanding. Mr. Robinson's job allowed him to provide a decent standard of living for himself and his family. Even after he was diagnosed with a serious illness, he continued to be able to work.

Years earlier, he had served his country ably in the military. He was also a talented athlete and had been a boxer as a young man. But when Michelle was a young girl, Fraser Robinson contracted multiple sclerosis, a crippling disease that affects the muscles of the body. For most of the time Michelle knew her father, Mr. Robinson limped and, later, needed a cane to get around.

From her father, young Michelle learned the lesson that she could achieve whatever she wished to in her life if she worked hard enough at it. "Because when you see a father like mine, a man with a disability . . . he couldn't walk without the assistance of a cane," she recalled. "But he got up and went to work every day. That's what I saw." He was "a man who didn't complain, was never late, never expressed any level of doubt about his situation in his life, and taught us that we could dream of anything."

There was no doubt in Michelle's mind that her father had selflessly put off his own dreams. He did this so that she and her brother could achieve whatever they dared to hope for. "That is what gave him his hope," she said. "He had long since put down his hopes and dreams for his own life." Michelle's father was a man whose life of hard work and suffering had not been in vain because of what he could give to her and her family: "By getting up and going to work every day, and keeping a roof over our heads, and being diligent and honest, he put two kids through Princeton. Imagine that."

Fraser Robinson served as a role model for being a tireless and uncomplaining hard worker. Michelle would take on these characteristics herself later in life. Fraser Robinson would also provide a glimpse into a world that would be very much a part of his daughter's life: politics.

When he was first married, Fraser Robinson became involved with the local Democratic Party—a very powerful force in Chicago both then and now. Even though he was only a volunteer, Mr. Robinson eventually became a precinct captain, an important position in the party. In this role, he would do such hands-on duties as going door-to-door, handing out information, and chatting with neighbors. It was his job to get to know and understand the concerns of the voters within his area. Naturally, as a precinct captain, Fraser Robinson was also expected to encourage the people to turn out and vote for the Democratic candidates who ran for election in the district.

Michelle's mother, Marian (born Shields), was also a hard worker and a role model for Michelle. Before Marian had children, she was employed as a secretary at various businesses. She quit her job to become a stay-at-home mother. She ran the Robinson household and also tutored Michelle and her older brother. Marian Robinson was such a good teacher that both children learned to read before they entered elementary school.

In his book *The Audacity of Hope*, Barack Obama describes how involved Michelle's mother was in her children's education. "There was Marian, the pretty, sensible mother who baked birthday cakes, kept order in the house, and had volunteered at school to make sure her children were behaving and that the teachers were doing what they were supposed to be doing."

Michelle's parents were married in 1960. Both had grown up in the same South Side neighborhood where they eventually chose to raise their own family. Two years after her brother, Craig, was born, Michelle LaVaughn arrived on January 17, 1964.

The family occupied a small apartment on the upper floor of a brick house at 7436 South Euclid Avenue, on Chicago's South Side. Then, as now, the South Side was a lower- to middle-class neighborhood where both the poor and the more affluent lived together. The region did have some grim pockets of poverty, especially in its public housing projects.

But the University of Chicago was nearby, and the school helped to attract a mix of black and white professionals, as well as working-class families like the Robinsons, to the neighborhood.

The apartment, which was owned by Michelle Obama's great-aunt, had one bedroom. Michelle's parents shared this room. To give Michelle and her brother, Craig, their own bedrooms, the living room was divided into three compartments. The third space was kept as a living room and study where schoolwork—a big priority in the Robinson household—could be done.

Everyone in the family shared one bathroom. This was the bathroom that young "Miche" (the nickname Craig gave her) had to clean. In the Robinson household, both children had chores. Every Saturday, Michelle had to clean the bathroom. She scrubbed the sink, mopped the floor, and cleaned the toilet. The children also had to help out in the kitchen. "We alternated washing dishes," said Craig. "I had Monday, Wednesday, Friday. Michelle had Tuesday, Thursday, Saturday."

The Robinsons owned a television set, but the children had very limited access. However, this careful monitoring didn't keep quick-witted Michelle from staying up-to-date on the latest television shows of her day. When Craig introduced her at the Democratic National Convention in August 2008, he said, "This is the person who—even though we were allowed only one hour of television a night—somehow managed to commit to memory every episode of *The Brady Bunch*."

Providing a rare inside view of his sister as an impatient young girl, Craig Robinson also said, "It's funny to think that this is the same person who used to wake me up early—and I mean *early*—on Christmas morning, because we both had to be up at the same time in order to open our presents." Craig, who won a basketball scholarship to college and would go on to have a successful career coaching that sport, also mentioned that she was "the person who would play the piano to calm me down before all of my big games in high school."

Michelle was close to her brother growing up. Craig was avid about playing sports, and Michelle would, on occasion, show up on the basketball court to play with her brother and his friends. Long-limbed and tall at five feet, eleven inches, she was a keen competitor when she set her mind to it. Perhaps to avoid comparisons with her brother, she generally avoided playing team sports. Instead, she followed more solitary pursuits like playing the piano, reading, and writing short stories in a spiral notebook.

Michelle looked up to her brother, both when they were children and also as adults. As she said in her speech at the Democratic National Convention, "I come here as a sister, blessed with my brother, who is my mentor, my protector, and my lifelong friend." Elsewhere, she has said that she looks up to him, and she means *up*—he stands six feet, six inches tall.

When she was young, Michelle loved playing with "girl" stuff, too. As one childhood friend recalled, "She set up an Easy-Bake Oven in her bedroom." (This popular toy stove actually cooked simple recipes with a burning pellet of fuel.) She also liked to play with dolls. Her friend remembers Michelle "sprawled across the carpet with the African-American version of Barbie, her mate, Ken, their toy house, and car."

There was also time for games like chess and Monopoly. Michelle was a fierce competitor. When they played Monopoly together, Craig had to "let her win enough that she wouldn't quit." He further explained, "My sister is a poor sport. She doesn't like to lose."

Like most children, Michelle and her brother may

have acted up or misbehaved in some way. When this happened, according to Michelle, her father would never shout or even raise his voice. Instead, he would give them a cold stare and say, "I'm disappointed." This would cause young Michelle and her brother to burst into tears. "You never wanted to disappoint him," she said. "We would be bawling."

When schoolwork and games were put aside, there was always good conversation around the dinner table. Marian Robinson was a capable cook and provided a good homemade dinner for the family every night. Michelle and her brother would talk about some of the events of their day, perhaps something particularly interesting that they had learned in school or that they had done that afternoon.

Everyone participated in the lively discussions around the table. Michelle was articulate, and her verbal skills would help her later in life when she worked as a lawyer and businesswoman. When Michelle graduated from Harvard Law School in 1988, perhaps her parents had these early family debates in mind when they took out a small ad in the yearbook. It said, "We knew you would do this fifteen years ago when we could never make you shut up."

Other members of the extended Robinson family

occasionally joined in the fun, too. In *The Audacity of Hope*, Barack Obama described the festive atmosphere in the house. "And there were uncles and aunts and cousins everywhere, stopping by to sit around the kitchen table and eat until they burst and tell wild stories and listen to Grandpa's old jazz collection and laugh deep into the night."

Growing up in a happy home would have long-lasting effects on the adults that Michelle and her brother would become. Craig Robinson shared his perspective of their childhood with a journalist at the *Washington Post*: "When you grow up as a black kid in a white world, so many times people are telling you, sometimes not maliciously, sometimes maliciously, you're not good enough. To have a family who constantly reminded you how smart you were, how good you were, how pleasant it was to be around you, how successful you could be, it's hard to combat."

Speaking for both himself and his sister, Craig added, "Our parents gave us a little head start by making us feel confident. It sounds so corny, but that's how we grew up."

Michelle, too, has said that she had been raised to look at the world as one full of possibilities and not to think about all the things that might stand in her way. "My parents told us time and time again, 'Don't tell us what you can't do,' " she said. " 'And don't worry what can go wrong.' " Michelle has tried to live by this advice ever since.

3 School Days

Both Michelle Robinson and her brother, Craig, were highly motivated students. Craig recounts, "Without being immodest, we were always smart, we were always driven, and we were always encouraged to do the best you can do, not just what's necessary." In the Robinson household, that same encouragement applied to education. Although neither parent went to college, both children were well aware of the goal of higher education. "And when it came to going to schools, we all wanted to go to the best schools we could," said Craig.

For Michelle, this excellence in schools began at the Bryn Mawr Public Elementary School. Michelle developed good study skills at an early age, and nurtured and encouraged by her parents, she did so well that she skipped second grade. Young Michelle was following a family tradition: Her brother and *both* parents also had skipped second grade! Intelligence ran in the family.

Clearly, both the example her hardworking parents set and the expectations they held for their daughter had their effect. When asked many years later what her parents would have done if she had brought home anything less than an A grade, Michelle shrugged. "I don't know," she replied, "because they never had to deal with that." Michelle worked hard so she would never disappoint the parents who had given her so much.

Getting good grades in school was extremely important for the Robinson children. However, from a young age they were also taught that there were other priorities to keep in mind. "More important, even, than learning to read and write was to teach them to think," Mrs. Robinson said. "We told them, 'Make sure you respect your teachers, but don't hesitate to question them. Don't even allow us to just say anything to you. Ask us why.'"

Although things went generally smoothly at Michelle's elementary school (as those A's mounted up), there must have been some early indication of the steely resolve that would reveal itself in the grown woman. As an old law school friend recalls, "I remember Michelle telling me about a teacher complaining about her temper in elementary school. She said her mom told the teacher, 'Yeah, she's got a temper. But we decided to keep her anyway!'"

In 1975, when Michelle was in sixth grade, the elementary school she attended was given a grant to start a "gifted student" program. Michelle was selected to participate in the program. She would have an opportunity to take advanced courses such as biology and French at Kennedy-King, the local community college.

The difference between these classes and the ones ordinary students were taking soon became obvious. In the science class, for instance, Michelle and her classmates dissected rat specimens to see how the muscles of the animal were formed and how they worked. This provided them with practical hands-on experience. On a more theoretical level, the students studied advanced subjects such as photosynthesis, exploring the cellular interaction with light that is the basis for all plant life. As a friend of Michelle's later said, "This is not what normal seventh graders were getting."

Michelle graduated with honors from the Bryn Mawr Public Elementary School in 1977. The question of where she would now attend high school was an important one. Michelle and her parents discussed the possibilities. There were high schools that were located fairly close to the Robinson home, but another option presented itself: the chance to attend a new kind of school, a magnet high school.

For years, resentment among African Americans had been growing in response to what was seen as a double standard in education for blacks versus whites in towns and cities around the country. Black schools lacked books, supplies, and resources and provided far fewer advantages than the schools in mainly white neighborhoods. In the 1960s in Chicago, this situation had led to protests, sometimes violent, to change the policies that left poorer black communities with understaffed schools. .

The solution was to form secondary schools, called magnet schools, that had dedicated, highly trained teachers who would have access to better equipment and facilities. These high schools would be available to qualified students regardless of their race. They would feature clubs and extracurricular opportunities not generally seen in ordinary schools. Students lucky enough to attend a magnet school would have many advantages, including, perhaps, a chance for admittance to a top-rated college after graduation.

In the fall of 1977, Michelle Robinson entered ninth grade at the Whitney M. Young Magnet High School. She was now part of an elite group of boys and girls from all over the city, from all different backgrounds and races. All of them had one thing in common: They wanted to *learn*.

According to the official mission statement of the Whitney M. Young Magnet High School, the purpose of the school is to "create a positive, diverse, friendly, and challenging learning community where students grow toward fulfilling their potential in academic, artistic, physical, and socio-emotional dimensions. We value the uniqueness of each student and prepare our graduates both to succeed in their own lives and to make positive contributions to society." Michelle certainly lived up to the ideals held by the school.

Although there was a public high school just one block away from the Robinson home, Michelle's parents encouraged her to make the long trip back and forth to her new school. Michelle was cheerful about the rigors of the trip, even on days when the cold winds blew off Lake Michigan and the buses were delayed by snowdrifts. Once she got to her new school, Michelle found a warm and welcoming environment where she thrived both academically and socially.

"When she applied and came here, the tradition of leaving one's neighborhood to go to high school was very new, and a person had to be gutsy to do it. For most kids who came here in those times, the idea that you would take two or three buses and a train to come here was a very new idea," said Dagny Bloland, a teacher who taught at the school in the 1980s.

Furthermore, said Bloland, the school wasn't in the most attractive part of the city. "It was an industrial neighborhood, with factories, sometimes abandoned. The stores weren't here yet, and the churches were not thriving. It was a real experiment to come here. I think you had to be the sort of person and the sort of family that would put education above everything else." The Robinsons were just such a family.

At Whitney, young Michelle had no trouble making friends. Although academic studies were taken seriously, by many accounts the school had a happy atmosphere that seemed free of the racial tension that existed in high schools in other parts of Chicago. The students came from widely different backgrounds, but they seemed to be united by the common pursuit of the best education and all the advantages they would gain.

There must have been tensions—it was a high school, after all—but they weren't caused by racial issues. Said one classmate of Michelle's, "Although it was racially diverse, the school was not racially divided. It was a melting pot. Our homecoming court was black and white. There was no racial undertone. Everything was just, I don't know, harmonious. Sports and everything. We had two Chinese guys who were phenomenal basketball players."

If Michelle felt any tension, it probably arose from her constant striving for academic excellence. Her mother, Marian, recalled young Michelle being frustrated about not doing well on tests. "She was disappointed with herself," she said. "She used to have a little bit of trouble with tests, so she did whatever she had to, to make up for that."

Mrs. Robinson also mentioned the sibling rivalry between her children. "I'm sure it was psychological, because she was hardworking and she had a brother who could pass a test just by carrying a book under his arm. When you are around someone like that, even if you are okay, you want to be as good or better."

Michelle made the honor roll all four years that she attended Whitney Young. She had successfully taken and passed advanced placement classes. She was a member of the National Honor Society. Along with her high academic achievement, she excelled in extracurricular activities. She was student council treasurer and a member of the fundraising publicity committee.

All these accomplishments made her an attractive and strong candidate for college. But could she reach the top? Could she get into an Ivy League college?

Despite her hard work and dedication, Michelle was not at the top of her class at Whitney Young. Although she studied hard, she had a little trouble scoring well on tests. Some of her teachers told her she wasn't quite cut out for a top-tier school like Princeton, even though her brother had been accepted there. Her brother was a top student, *and* he had been a terrific basketball player in high school. Later, Michelle would observe that "Princeton, the Ivy Leagues swoop up kids" such as her brother, Craig. "A black kid from the South Side of Chicago who plays basketball and is smart," she added. "He was getting in everywhere."

Craig's admission into Princeton just made

Michelle even more determined. As she saw it, she deserved to get into that college, too. "I *knew* him, and I knew his study habits, and I was like, 'I can do that, too.'"

Craig has admitted as much himself in an interview, saying, "Michelle works harder than anyone I know." He reminisced about a common scene from their childhood. "I'd come home from basketball practice, and she'd be working. I'd sit down on the sofa and watch TV; she'd keep working. When I turned off the TV, she'd still be working."

In the end, Michelle applied to Princeton—and was accepted. Now the goal that she had striven for, the one that her parents had sacrificed and prayed for, was about to be reached. In the fall of 1981, Michelle Robinson would attend one of the most prestigious colleges in the country.

4 Princeton University

Aside from the question of whether she was really smart enough to attend an Ivy League school, other factors may have caused some uneasiness. For seventeen-year-old Michelle, Princeton University was a formidable adjustment. Located in a leafy green New Jersey suburb with gray, Gothic granite buildings scattered amid carefully tended lawns and shrubs, the campus must have looked somewhat strange to a girl from Chicago's South Side.

Also, in the year Michelle entered Princeton, minority students made up only 16 percent of the college's population. Instead of the overwhelmingly black neighborhoods that she had grown up in, for the first time in her life Michelle would confront what it really meant to be a *minority*. She never complained to her parents about any misgivings she may have had. "She didn't talk about it a lot," said her mother, Marian. "I just learned from reading some articles that she did feel like she was different from other people. But she never let that bother her."

By 1981, when Michelle began attending college, there were few outward signs of racism at Princeton. The obvious discriminatory practice of prohibiting African Americans from attending the college was a distant memory. Even in the South, segregation, or the separation by race enforced by Jim Crow laws, had ended in the 1950s. Nonetheless, there were still aspects of the school that made the girl from the South Side feel like an outsider.

One of Princeton's oldest traditions, the "eating clubs," still existed as a mainly whites-only institution on campus. These members-only organizations were somewhat like fraternities. They could be joined by invitation only. There were alternatives—no one starved at Princeton—but a minority student was far less likely to be asked to join an eating club. An eating club was more than just a place to eat your meals. These clubs served as social hubs. They often sponsored parties, dances, and other events where students could meet one another.

An often-told story concerns the day Michelle arrived at her Princeton dorm room her freshman year. Upon seeing Michelle, or at least her *color*, the mother of one of her white roommates rushed to the campus housing office to demand that her daughter be moved immediately. The woman was from the South, and to her prejudiced way of thinking, having her daughter living in the same room as a black girl was unthinkable. It's not clear whether Michelle knew that this had happened at the time, but it illustrates the attitude toward blacks by at least some of her classmates.

There were other, more subtle ways in which some students were made to feel inferior. Angela Acree, one of Michelle's best friends at Princeton and her roommate, said that many white students couldn't hide their feelings that most black classmates didn't deserve to be at Princeton. They thought that African-American students had been admitted only because of affirmative action. They felt this policy gave preference to black students. According to Angela Acree, black students would be ignored on campus by white students they knew from class. "It was, like, here comes a black kid," she said.

Michelle had certainly known classmates and friends back in Chicago who were more well-to-do than her family. Still, seeing some of the wealth displayed by some of the other Princeton students was a surprise. "I remember being shocked," she said, "by students who drove BMWs. I didn't even know *parents* who drove BMWs."

Michelle's dorm room decor also looked different from that of the rooms of wealthier students. Lauren Collins, her roommate for three years, said, "We couldn't afford any furniture, so we just had pillows on the floor, and a stereo." (Apparently, Michelle was known for her collection of Stevie Wonder records.) Money may have been tight, but it didn't stop Michelle from looking her best. According to her friend Angela, Michelle was "always fashionably dressed, even on a budget. You wouldn't catch her in sweats, even back then."

If black students felt unwelcome at the more mainstream social events at Princeton, there were places they could go where they felt more at home. One of them was the Third World Center, where Michelle and her black friends socialized. According to Angela, "The white people didn't dance—I know that sounds like a cliché—and they also played a completely different kind of music, whereas we were playing R & B, Luther Vandross, Run-DMC at the Third World Center."

Michelle was a sociology major at Princeton. Her senior thesis was titled "Princeton-Educated Blacks and the Black Community." To research her topic, Michelle sent out hundreds of questionnaires to black graduates of Princeton asking them about how they felt toward white people both before and after attending college.

Also, Michelle asked them how their experience at Princeton made them feel about themselves and their relationship with other African Americans. It's not hard to see that these were questions Michelle was asking herself at the time.

In the introduction to her thesis, Michelle wonders what impact a particular college experience would have on black students. "As more blacks begin attending predominantly white universities, it will be helpful to know how their experiences in these universities affect their future attitudes. In years to come, if their attitudes do change, is it possible, for example, that they will become more comfortable interacting with blacks or with whites in various activities? Will they become more or less motivated to benefit the black community?" Perhaps Michelle, the girl from the South Side, was also trying to figure out what was going to become of her.

Michelle may have wondered what convictions would shape her future, but Michelle still had her feet firmly on the ground. She was confident and comfortable with where she had come from. Michelle dedicated her thesis to her family and friends: "To Mom, Dad, Craig, and all of my special friends: Thank you for loving me and always making me feel good about myself."

Perhaps most revealing of all are the words Michelle wrote about her perception of her race as a factor in her academic life. Looking back on almost four years spent at college, she writes in her thesis, "My experiences at Princeton have made me far more aware of my 'blackness' than ever before. I have found that at Princeton no matter how liberal and open-minded some of my white professors and classmates try to be toward me, I sometimes feel like a visitor on campus, as if I really don't belong. Regardless of the circumstances under which I interact with whites at Princeton, it often seems as if, to them, I will always be black first and a student second."

Michelle graduated cum laude (Latin for "with honors") in 1985. In the fall, she would attend another old-line Ivy League institution: Harvard Law School.

5 Harvard Law School

In the fall of 1985, Michelle Robinson entered Harvard Law School in Cambridge, Massachusetts. The institution was founded in 1817. It has produced some of this country's finest lawyers, many of whom have risen to important positions in business and government. Graduates of Harvard Law School have served in the U.S. Senate and on the Supreme Court.

Harvard was one of the best law schools in the country. Michelle had worked hard at Princeton and graduated with departmental honors. There was no doubt in her mind that she had earned her place at Harvard Law School. Michelle was focused and goal-oriented. In a way, she had revealed her ambition in her Princeton thesis.

More than a year before entering Harvard, she wrote, "For example, as I enter my final year at Princeton, I find myself striving for many of the same goals as my white classmates—acceptance to a prestigious graduate or professional school."

Charles J. Ogletree, Michelle's academic adviser at Harvard Law, said, "Princeton was a real crossroads of identity for Michelle." He felt her experience at college had presented her with important questions about her background and education. She wondered, *Who am I?* or, put another way, "whether I retain my identity given by my African-American parents, or whether the education from an elite university has transformed me into something different than what they made me." But did it have to be just one or the other?

According to Ogletree, Michelle had come to a conclusion in her four years at Princeton. "By the time she got to Harvard, she had answered the question. She could be both brilliant and black."

This new sense of confidence was apparent to others. A classmate of Michelle's at Harvard Law School described her this way: "She has incredible presence. . . . She's very, very smart, very charismatic, very well spoken."

The ability to state an argument or legal position clearly is an important part of being a successful lawyer. Lawyers must not only know the law but also be good speakers and be able to present strong arguments. In many ways, law school tries to imitate the circumstances that will be found in the real legal world. To this end, students at Harvard Law School are encouraged to develop debating skills that will help them convincingly argue cases before a judge and jury.

Michelle Robinson earned the respect of her family for her persistence in making her "case" around the dinner table back in Chicago. How did she do in the competitive arena of Harvard Law School?

"Michelle was a student in my legal profession class, in which I ask students how they would react to difficult ethical and professional challenges," said Professor David B. Wilkins. "Not surprisingly, many students shy away from putting themselves on the line in this way, preferring to hedge their bets or deploy technical arguments that seem to absolve them from the responsibilities of decision making. Michelle had no need for such fig leaves." Rather, he said, "she always stated her position clearly and decisively."

Time is very precious to a law student. Michelle spent many hours studying such subjects as criminal and contract law cases and theory. But she also found the time to become very involved in community service, working for a Harvard-run organization that provided legal help to poor people in the surrounding community.

If tenants were being unfairly evicted, they could ask the Harvard Legal Aid Bureau for advice in fighting the landlord. Women who couldn't afford a lawyer could get help filing for divorce or getting custody of their children. Ronald Torbert, a classmate who worked with Michelle at the bureau, said, "We got to do the kind of work we thought we came to law school eventually to do, but we were also working with real people."

Students who worked for legal aid spent a lot of hours there, and Torbert remembers Michelle clearly from those days. "She was very mature, very bright. She handled some of the more complex landlord-and-tenant issues. I just remember her being very serious about the work she did, and she really cared about the people she worked with."

As she had been at Princeton, Michelle got

involved in African-American organizations at Harvard Law, too. One such group was the Black Law Students Association. One of the organization's activities was to arrange meetings with black Harvard alumni. Students wanted to know about the careers alumni pursued with their law degrees after graduation. Some spoke of their work as lawyers in private practice. Others told of working for the government or in various community-oriented organizations.

What would Michelle do after graduation from Harvard Law? She had been contemplating this decision for a long time. In her Princeton thesis, she wrote that "it is conceivable that my four years of exposure to a predominantly white, Ivy League university has instilled within me certain conservative values," which would lead her to seek "a high-paying position in a successful corporation."

Harvard Law, like most law schools, allowed recruitment on campus. Corporate firms of all sizes and types would come to Cambridge and try to lure graduates with promises of interesting and financially rewarding work. With mounting student loans dragging her down in debt, Michelle did what many of her classmates did: She joined a private practice law firm. Aside from the high salary she would earn, the firm offered her a benefit beyond riches. It would take her back to her family and her hometown of Chicago.

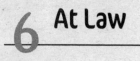

6 At Law

In 1988, Michelle Robinson started full-time work in the Chicago office of Sidley Austin, a large corporate law firm. Sidley Austin does legal work for all different kinds of people and companies, who are called clients. The law firm oversees many different aspects of its clients' dealings.

If a client wants to buy property, the law firm makes sure that the building or land is legally available to be sold. If a client enters into an agreement with another company for business reasons, the firm writes the contract that will make sure the deal is legally valid. Clients may even need a law firm's help in writing a will that legally provides for their wishes. These are the types of skills that Michelle learned at Harvard Law School. In our developed society, it's hard to find an aspect of life that isn't affected in some way by laws and lawyers.

Michelle first went to work at Sidley Austin when she was a student at Harvard Law School. She was hired to work during the summer as a "summer associate." Most law firms have such temporary positions. They provide well-paying jobs to students and benefit from gaining the assistance of a bright, hardworking staff. They also provide an opportunity to see if there is a good fit between employer and employee, which may lead to a permanent job. Michelle liked the summer work she did at Sidley Austin. When she was offered a position after graduating from Harvard, she accepted.

Michelle joined the marketing division at Sidley Austin. This department of the firm specialized in law that pertained to entertainment. The marketing division's job was to make sure that its clients had fair and profitable dealings with the companies they worked with. One such client was the flamboyant boxing promoter Don King, who was based in Chicago. Another client was Coors Brewing Company, which needed legal advice regarding its television commercials and other advertising.

Whether through luck or preference, Michelle had landed in the least boring, most creative group in the firm. According to Mary Carragher, the lawyer who was her supervisor, "It was the most fun area of practice in the firm, bar none." Describing what she saw as a desirable assignment, she added, "We were the coolest people, and we had the best work. It was all popular culture stuff. You could do a lot of dull things in law, and this was and still is, in my opinion, the best stuff."

Another account the firm had was the company that held the rights to the giant purple dinosaur of public television, Barney. In time, Barney would become the best friend of millions of preschoolers around the country. People in the management of Sidley Austin knew that Michelle had worked on public interest cases in the past and that she had helped champion good causes. They thought assigning her to the Barney case would be a good fit.

Michelle "had very little experience in that area," said a supervisor at the time, "but she latched onto it and did a very good job with it."

But despite working on what "fun" accounts the firm had to offer, Michelle seemed unhappy with the assignments she was given. While working on the Coors account, Michelle complained that the nature of her work wasn't "interesting enough." Her boss, Quincy White, recalled, "She was extremely ambitious and wanted something that pushed her harder, something that was a more general challenge." Concluding that Michelle had higher standards for what made for satisfying work, he said, "I couldn't give her something that would meet her sense of ambition to change the world."

The idea that she might play a role that would help "change the world" would soon begin to take on new possibilities for Michelle. In the summer of 1988, she was given a seemingly routine assignment at Sidley Austin. Michelle Robinson was asked to be a mentor, a kind of adviser, to a young first-year law student with the unusual name of Barack Hussein Obama.

7 Meeting Barack

When she was first assigned to be a mentor to the man who would be her future husband—and president of the United States—Michelle was less than enthusiastic about the idea. She had already heard some things about Barack. Some of the lawyers at Sidley Austin had praised his "brilliant" introductory memo. Others lawyers were impressed by the outstanding first-year performance by the Harvard Law student. Even the secretaries (who had scoped him out during his previous interview) were saying how handsome he was.

Michelle was skeptical. "He sounded too good to be true," she said. "I had dated a lot of brothers who had this kind of reputation coming in, so I figured he was one of these smooth brothers who could talk straight and impress people," she commented dismissively.

But Michelle had a job to do. She showed Barack his office, reviewed some of the office procedures, and later, "we had lunch, and he had this bad sport jacket and a cigarette dangling from his mouth, and I thought, 'Oh, here you go. Here's this good-looking, smooth-talking guy. I've been down this road before.' "

For his part, Barack Obama was immediately smitten by Michelle. He later said that he liked that "she knew how to laugh, brightly and easily. . . . And there was something else, a glimmer that danced across her round, dark eyes whenever I looked at her, the slightest hint of uncertainty, as if, deep inside, she knew how fragile things were, and that if she ever let go, even for a moment, all her plans might quickly unravel. That touched me somehow, that trace of vulnerability. I wanted to know that part of her."

Michelle's role was to be an adviser to Barack, and they worked closely together. They saw each other every day that summer. They met either at the office or at one of the many outings arranged by the firm to promote good relations among coworkers.

The two of them went to a few parties together, and Barack remembers that Michelle "even tried to set me up with a couple of her friends. Still, she refused to go out on a proper date. It wasn't appropriate, she said, since she was my adviser."

But Barack had definitely caught Michelle's attention. As she told Katie Couric in a television interview years later, "Immediately I liked him because he didn't take himself too seriously, but he was very bright, had a very interesting background, just a good guy to talk to. You know, you could laugh easily with him. So I was, like, 'This is a friend.' "

Eventually, Barack, who wanted more than just friendship, as he put it, "wore her down." Not with flowers and candy and fancy dinners, though. Instead, Barack took Michelle to a Sunday morning meeting at a church on Chicago's South Side in the Altgeld Gardens neighborhood. It was one of the places he had worked when he had done his community service before going to law school. In that basement, where the audience was mostly filled with single African-American mothers, Michelle saw a "new" Barack—one who she liked *more* than just as a friend.

As Michelle watched Barack address that crowd, she was amazed "to see him transform himself from the guy who was a summer associate in a law firm with a suit, and then to come into this church basement with folks who were like me, who grew up like me, who were challenged and struggling in ways that I never would, and to be able to take off that suit and tie and become a whole 'nother person and connect with and feel comfortable in his own skin and to touch people's hearts in the way that he did, because people connected with his message."

Michelle realized that there was something special about Barack. She explained the feelings she had that day, saying, "People connected with his message. And I knew then and there there's something different about this guy. . . . Barack lived comfortably in those two worlds. And it was impressive. And his message was moving. I mean, it touched me. . . ."

Michelle and Barack spent their free time frequenting Michelle's childhood haunts and places that Barack had known from working in Chicago neighborhoods as a community organizer. The two of them had long conversations about what they had done in the past and what they hoped the future would hold.

From Michelle's point of view, the dashing man of mixed race must have seemed very exotic. In his book *The Audacity of Hope*, Barack writes about telling Michelle stories about living in Indonesia and what it was like to bodysurf on the beaches of Hawaii. She, in turn, explained to him what it was like growing up in Chicago and told him about the many good friends she had made there. She told him about her visit to Paris on a high school trip and how she got to use the French she had studied so hard to learn.

Company policy or not, the two were an item the rest of that summer. Barack even had a chance to meet the family that he knew was so important to Michelle.

Barack Obama was the son of a black father from Kenya and a white mother from Kansas. He scarcely knew his father, and when his mother went to Indonesia to live with her second husband, young Barack was left with his grandparents. They raised him on the island of Oahu in Hawaii. They provided him with a good home, and yet he never felt the closeness of a more traditional family.

In contrast, Barack said that "visiting the Robinson household was like dropping in on the set of *Leave It to Beaver.*" Barack was referring to the 1950s TV show about a happy all-American family who lived in an ideal world where it never seemed to rain and the biggest problem might be finding a lost kitten.

Barack immediately liked Michelle's father, Fraser Robinson. He described Mr. Robinson as "the kindly, good-humored father, who never missed a day of work or any of his son's ball games." And Marian was "pretty and sensible, who baked birthday cakes and kept order in the house." Although he would tease Michelle about her television-perfect family, it was clear that Barack enjoyed their company.

Of course the Robinsons had problems, too. One was the crippling illness that affected Michelle's father and the strain his condition put on the family. As Barack came to learn about multiple sclerosis, he saw "the hidden toll that her father's illness had taken on her family." Barack admired the courage and fortitude of the husband and father who "had carried out his responsibilities to his family without a trace of self-pity, giving himself an extra hour every morning to get to work, struggling with every physical act from driving a car to buttoning his shirt, smiling and joking as he labored."

But beyond the adversity the family faced together, Barack immediately saw the genuine warmth and love that existed in the close-knit Robinson household. Barack noted the contrast of the tight-knit Robinson family with his own. He observed, "For someone like me, who had barely known his father, who had spent much of his life traveling from place to place, his bloodlines scattered to the four winds, the home that Fraser and Marian Robinson built for themselves and their children stirred a longing for stability and a sense of place that I had not realized was there."

For their part, Michelle's parents liked the interesting young man who had come into their daughter's life. Marian remembers Barack as being polite and low-key. "He didn't talk about himself," she recollected. Referring to the challenges that awaited him back at law school, she said, "He didn't tell us that he was running for president of the *Harvard Law Review*. We never realized that he was as bright as he was."

But there was still one other Robinson family member to pass judgment on Barack that summer: Michelle's big brother, Craig. This was the brother who had preceded Michelle to Princeton, where he excelled at basketball and became one of the Ivy League's top scorers at the time. Craig was good enough to get drafted by the Philadelphia 76ers and then play professionally in Europe for a time. Later, Craig left a successful career in finance to coach college basketball, most recently as the head coach at the University of Oregon.

How did Craig go about sizing up his sister's new boyfriend? On the basketball court, of course. Barack was not as talented as the former Ivy League star and "pro" player, but Barack had never been shy about his "game," and he willingly got on the court with his future brother-in-law. Craig was impressed. He commented, "Barack's game is just like his personality—he's confident, not afraid to shoot the ball when he's open. See, that says a lot about a guy." He added, "A lot of guys wanna just be out there to say they were out there. But he wants to be out there and be a part of the game. He wants to try and win, and he wants to try and contribute."

Although there had been no "official" declarations of intent on either part, Michelle and Barack both now felt committed to each other as a couple who were exclusively dating each other. But when the summer was over, they would no longer be in the same city. Barack returned to Cambridge, Massachusetts, where he had two more years of law school to complete. Michelle continued working at Sidley Austin in Chicago.

8 Michelle Robinson and Barack Obama

Barack Obama had excelled in his first year at Harvard Law School. Perhaps his greatest achievement came in his second year, when he was elected president of the *Harvard Law Review*. This student-run journal is widely considered the most influential law publication in the country.

Just to be on the staff of the *Review* is an honor that only a small percentage of Harvard Law School's students can hope for. To be the president is the single greatest position a student can attain. Barack was the first African American to win the coveted title, an unprecedented achievement.

Initially, Barack was not sure he wanted the job. It was an exhausting job to run for the position. He also thought that it would do little to advance his career as a lawyer. However, during the process of getting elected, Barack learned some valuable lessons in dealing with opposing sides. Students who were liberal disagreed with those who were conservative. Blacks had priorities that were different from their white classmates'.

Barack learned these lessons from competing for the presidency of the *Harvard Law Review*. In the years to come, that same knowledge would provide him with important insights in his political career. First as an Illinois state senator, then as a U.S. senator, and finally as a candidate for the presidency of the United States, the experience Barack gained at Harvard Law School would prove to be invaluable.

There was also a more direct result of his success. His newfound fame eventually led to a contract to write *Dreams from My Father*, the book that would help both further his political career as well as establish his financial stability.

Meanwhile, back in Chicago, Michelle continued to work at Sidley Austin, although she was finding work as a corporate lawyer less and less satisfying. As she told *Newsweek* magazine, "I didn't see a whole lot of people who were just thrilled to be there. I met people who thought this was a good life. But were people waking up just bounding out of bed to get to work? No."

Michelle still lived in the apartment on the South Side with her family. She and Barack fell into the rhythm of a long-distance relationship. They exchanged letters and phone calls, and occasionally, on long weekends or holidays, they would get together either in Cambridge or Chicago.

Then, a terrible tragedy struck the Robinson family. Michelle's father, Fraser, died after suffering complications following kidney surgery. Although her father had been ill for much of his life, his death was unexpected. The Robinson family was devastated. Barack flew to Chicago to be with Michelle.

As Barack stood at the gravesite beside Michelle, he realized the personal commitment he felt toward Michelle. "Michelle's head [was] on my shoulder. As the casket was lowered, I promised Fraser Robinson that I would take care of his girl." Although he had known Michelle less than a year, he had already had a premonition of the future. He had come to the realization that, "in some unspoken, still tentative way, she and I were already becoming a family."

Her father's death caused Michelle to ask herself hard questions. She wondered whether she had chosen her career path wisely. As she related to *The New York Times*, when her father died, "I looked out at my neighborhood and sort of had an epiphany that I had to bring my skills to bear in the place that made me. I wanted to have a career motivated by passion and not just money." Michelle wanted her day-to-day work to do some greater good for others.

Around this time, another sad event occurred in Michelle's life. A close friend of hers from college, Suzanne Alele, died from cancer at age twenty-five. Before the onset of her illness, Suzanne had been a happy, free-spirited young woman. She had traveled widely and had lived her life to the fullest. Thinking of her own life after Suzanne's funeral, Michelle asked herself, "If I died in four months, is this how I would have wanted to spend this time?"

Typical of Michelle, she didn't brood about the sorry state of her life. She took action. Soon after, in the summer of 1991, she left her job as a lawyer and accepted a position on the staff of Chicago mayor Richard Daley. Maybe Michelle remembered the satisfaction that her father had experienced as a Democratic Party precinct captain. She felt that her new job would begin to satisfy the urge she had to do something important in giving back to the community.

9 A New Direction

From the standpoint of her ex-employer, there was no question that Michelle would be missed. Said Newton Minow, one of her supervisors at Sidley Austin, "As far as the firm was concerned, we considered it a real loss. We thought she was going to eventually become partner and have a big role there."

The law firm was sorry to lose Michelle. The mayor's office welcomed Michelle with open arms. The woman who hired her, Valerie Jarrett, then deputy chief of staff to Mayor Daley, recalled, "I interviewed Michelle, and an introductory session turned into an hour and a half. I offered her a job at the end of the interview, which was totally inappropriate since it was the mayor's decision." Ms. Jarrett, apparently, had liked Michelle's style. "She was so confident and committed and extremely open."

Before she accepted the offer, Michelle took the unusual step of asking Barack—now her fiancé—to meet with her prospective employer. The meeting went extremely well, and each was mutually impressed with the other. In fact, years later, Ms. Jarrett accepted a role as a senior adviser to Barack Obama's presidential campaign.

By accepting the job in the mayor's office, Michelle took a significant decrease in salary. On the upside, this would be her entry into the field of public service, an area that would prove to be central to her career. Soon after she was hired, Michelle was made the economic development coordinator of the city's department of planning and development.

In her new job, Michelle's responsibility was to find ways to help businesses in the city of Chicago to prosper. By understanding and interpreting the civil rules and regulations that applied, Michelle acted as a coordinator between the city's administration and the men and women who sought opportunities to grow their businesses.

Although Michelle lacked experience in the field

of economic development, she used the business knowledge she had acquired at the law firm to act as a kind of troubleshooter. In this role, she was able to size up a problem or situation quickly, and then competently see it through to its resolution. "She had this incredible ability to be a problem solver," said a colleague of Michelle's at the time. "She was just totally unflappable."

Michelle and Barack had continued to see each other during this period. They started discussing marriage, but nothing concrete developed. Apparently, there was a slight difference of opinion on the subject.

As Michelle said in an interview with *The New Yorker* magazine, "We would have this running debate throughout our relationship about whether marriage was necessary. It was sort of a bone of contention, because I was like, 'Look, buddy, I'm not one of those who'll just hang out forever.' You know, that's just not who I am." Michelle continued her recollection of the conversation, voicing Barack's point of view. "He was like, 'Marriage, it doesn't mean anything, it's really how you feel.' And I was like, 'Yeah, right.'"

Things came to a head one night in 1991, while the two were out on a dinner date at Gordon's, a fancy restaurant in Chicago. According to Michelle, they were celebrating Barack's passing his bar exam, and he was going on at length repeating his dim view of marriage. But when dessert came out, there was a ring on the tray!

10 Marriage and Family

The couple was married in October 1992 at Trinity United Church of Christ by the Reverend Jeremiah Wright, and they held their reception at the South Shore Cultural Center. Santita Jackson, a longtime friend of Michelle's and daughter of the Reverend Jesse Jackson, sang at the wedding. After going on a honeymoon in California, Michelle and her new husband lived with her mother in Michelle's childhood home on the South Side.

Soon they moved to a small apartment of their own in the more upscale section of Chicago called Hyde Park. Michelle was still working for Mayor Daley's office. Barack was working at a small civil rights law firm and teaching at the University of Chicago Law

School. Barack looks back fondly at those days in *The Audacity of Hope*: "Mostly, though, those early years were full of ordinary pleasures—going to movies, having dinner with friends, catching the occasional concert."

It was while they lived in Hyde Park that Michelle switched jobs again. In the early 1990s, Barack was on the founding board of a nonprofit national service organization called Public Allies, whose mission was to train young people to serve in the area of public service. Later, it would become a part of the Clinton administration's AmeriCorps effort. Before he left in 1993, he recommended Michelle for the position of executive director.

In her customary fashion, Michelle jumped right into the demanding work with both feet. According to Julian Posada, her deputy director at Public Allies, "There was an intensity to her that, you know, this has got to work, this is a big vision, this isn't easy," he recalled. "Michelle's intensity was like: We have to deliver."

Referring to her previous employment, Posada added, "I'm sure she came from a lot more infrastructure. There was no sense that this was a plush law firm, that's all gone. It's like, 'Who's going to lick envelopes today?' Nothing was beneath her."

When recruitment of trainees was required, Michelle went canvassing door-to-door in Cabrini Green, a public housing project neighborhood with an unsafe reputation. She was also there when someone needed to tap wealthy donors and big foundations for donations to fund the program. Competing with other better-known causes, Michelle called on the connections she had made while working at the Sidley Austin law firm and Mayor Daley's office to obtain donations.

For her part, Michelle called her work with Public Allies "by far the best thing I've done in my professional career. It was the first thing that was mine, and I was responsible for every aspect of it." In a comment that most workers can only dream of saying, she admitted, "My passions and talents converged."

Her husband, Barack, was also keeping busy. In 1997, Barack ran for and won the election to become the Illinois state senator from Chicago's thirteenth district. The legislature is located in the state capital, Springfield, some two hundred miles from his home on the South Side. Barack really valued Michelle's support of his political career and the requirements of his new job. As he wrote in his book *The Audacity of Hope*, "Our time together got squeezed even more when I ran for the state legislature, but despite my lengthy absences and her general dislike of politics, Michelle supported the decision; 'I know it's something you want to do,' she would tell me."

In a touching revelation of their marriage, Barack wrote, "On the nights I was in Springfield, we'd talk and laugh over the phone, sharing the humor and frustrations of our days apart, and I would fall asleep content in the knowledge of our love."

At this point in time, Michelle and Barack discussed plans to start a family. With her typically forward thinking, Michelle realized that the consuming commitment she showed in her work at Public Allies would not be consistent with that goal. So, after finding and recruiting a replacement to head up Public Allies, Michelle started to look for part-time work that would be closer to their home in Hyde Park.

Although she had spent almost her whole life, apart from her university years, in the same neighborhood, incredibly, Michelle had never set foot on the campus of the University of Chicago. As she put it, "As a black kid on the South Side, the University of Chicago was a foreign entity to me." This changed in 1996, when she took a job as the associate dean of Student Services.

Once again, Michelle would use her considerable skills as a communicator and organizer. In this case, the goal was to involve University of Chicago students in the social issues of the surrounding neighborhood. Since Michelle grew up in that neighborhood, she was uniquely positioned to try to bridge the gap that existed between the two parties at that time.

In addition to external "bridge building" between the school and the community, Michelle also worked within the university in its effort to eliminate sexism on campus. A colleague who served with her on the sexual harassment policy committee said that the situation was a "highly charged environment, because it was complex cases tied to personalities." Regarding Michelle's role, he said, "She was great at it. She had a real directness and sense of humor—not bawdy, just a down-to-earth 'let's get this done.'"

Then, in 1999, on the Fourth of July, Malia Ann was born. Her adoring father described the moment in *The Audacity of Hope*: "So calm and so beautiful, with big hypnotic eyes that seemed to read the world the moment they opened." Michelle and Barack were thrilled with Malia, but her arrival would put even more pressure on the young couple.

Although Michelle's work at the University of Chicago was part-time, it still required a big commitment of time and effort. And Barack, when he wasn't attending to his responsibilities as a legislator, was working on his first book, *Dreams from My Father*.

Barack writes of the stress that existed then, and largely owns up to being a major contributor to the problem. "Partly because I was still working on my first book, and perhaps because I had lived most of my life an only child, I would often spend the evening holed up in my office in the back of our railroad apartment; what I considered normal often left Michelle feeling lonely."

Referring to the birth of their second daughter, Natasha (called Sasha), when Barack was more involved in politics than ever, he wrote, "My wife's anger toward me seemed barely contained. 'You only think of yourself,' she would tell me. 'I never thought I'd have to raise a family alone.'"

These accusations must have stung, but Barack writes that it was only with the passage of time that he truly credited his wife for the role she played in keeping the family together. "In the end," he wrote, "I credit Michelle's strength—her willingness to manage these tensions and sacrifices on behalf of the girls—with carrying us through the difficult times."

Later, in November 2004, Barack was elected a U.S. senator, representing the state of Illinois in Washington, D.C. This was a great step forward in Barack's career as a politician. However, it would put an even greater strain on the Obama family, as he would now have to fly back and forth to the nation's capital and stay at a small apartment there while Congress was in session.

As Michelle looks back, she says she just faced the fact that she had to make the best of the situation. She didn't really have a choice if her family were to remain healthy and stable. "I cannot be crazy, because then I'm a crazy mother and I'm an angry wife." Typical of the eminently sensible woman she is, Michelle did not dwell on the unjustness of her situation.

Instead, she readily saw how it wasn't just her problem but one that affects millions of women. As she told the *Chicago Tribune*, "What I notice about men, all men, is that their order is me, my family, God is in there somewhere, but me is first. And for women, me is fourth, and that's not healthy."

Part of Michelle's levelheaded way of dealing with the situation was to look for a new work challenge. A month after Sasha was born, she received a phone call about a job from the new president of the University of Chicago Medical Center. The position involved community outreach for the hospital—right up Michelle's alley.

She was reluctant at first, but after several friends encouraged her, she grudgingly agreed to meet the man offering the job. As she recalls, "People said, you really have to talk to this guy, he's great. So I'm thinking, I'll do this as a courtesy, demand a whole bunch of stuff he's not going to give me, he'll say no, and we'll be done."

Since many of her demands revolved around being the mother of a newborn child, she arrived at the interview with two-month-old Sasha slung in a baby carrier. As she recalls the interview with the hospital president, she said, "I had on a breastfeeding top. I strolled in, 'Hi! This is me! New baby!'" Michelle then went on to detail all her demands: total control over her schedule, big salary, adequate budget, and more. Furthermore she added, "I can't be in your office all afternoon in meetings. Also, I can't be your diversity—a nice person who could 'represent.'"

To her amazement, the president agreed to all her demands. "So I built this whole new arm of the hospital," she declared. Among her achievements was a new policy to allocate some of the hospital's funds to local providers of goods and services. Another was to look at race-based health issues in considering research projects at the institution. And Michelle enjoyed it every step of the way, as she notes: "When you go from nothing to something, that's fun."

One of the hospital's directors who reported to Michelle had this appraisal of her. "She has the ability to bring the best out in people," he said, "really tapping into what their strengths and gifts and talents are. It's inspiring."

Since 2005, the Obama home has been a historic Georgian-style revival mansion in Chicago's South Side. The three-story house in the fashionable Hyde Park neighborhood reportedly cost $1.6 million. The purchase was made possible largely from the proceeds of Barack Obama's bestselling books.

The previous year, Barack Obama had given the keynote speech at the 2004 Democratic National Convention in Boston, Massachusetts. Then a little-known junior senator, this inspiring speech, seen by millions, instantly turned Barack into a much-talked-about public figure. It kicked his political career into high gear and set the stage for his historic run for president. Another consequence was that it made a bestseller out of a book that had been out of print for years.

In 1995, Barack had written the book *Dreams from My Father: A Story of Race and Inheritance*. He was invited by the publisher to write the book largely because of the fame he had earned after becoming the first African-American president of the *Harvard Law Review*. When it was first published, it got fairly good reviews but sold very few copies.

After Barack gave the keynote speech, the enormous interest in him caused the book's sales to skyrocket. Since then, the book has continued to sell and generate profits. In 2006, Barack followed this book with another, titled *The Audacity of Hope: Thoughts on Reclaiming the American Dream*. It, too, has been and remains a bestseller.

This newfound source of wealth, aside from providing a comfortable home for the Obamas, would also have a direct impact on Barack's political fortune. Before he entered the race for president, Barack consulted with his wife. Amid other concerns that Michelle had, a central one was how this move would affect their financial security. Ever the practical wife and mother, Michelle had some hard questions for her ambitious husband.

"How do we manage this in terms of time? What happens to my career?" she asked. (At the time, Michelle was making more than $270,000 a year at her job with the University of Chicago—much more than her husband made as a U.S. senator.) "How are we going to manage this financially? What most people don't understand, politics is a millionaire's game. It requires you to have resources. Even being in the U.S. Senate, you've got to have a home in your home state and in Washington. You have to be able to afford two mortgages."

It wasn't only money matters that concerned Michelle. For her, family came first. "My comfort zone comes from understanding the plan," she explained. "How am I going to make my way through the many obstacles that will be there for myself individually, for my children, for us as a family?" She needed to know the nitty-gritty details. "Where are we going to live? Where would the kids go to school? For me it's all very practical, on-the-ground kinds of concerns."

The future First Lady got satisfactory answers to her questions, and the marathon race for the presidency looked like it was about to begin. Apparently, some of the reassurances she got from Barack came during their Christmas vacation that year. Later, she would tell a crowd in Iowa, "When you're on a beach in Hawaii, everything looks possible."

11 On the Campaign Trail

The long grind of the presidential campaign began in earnest in February 2007. Realistically assessing the situation, Michelle reduced her work schedule at the hospital to 20 percent by May. When even this became difficult, she took a leave of absence that would become more or less permanent.

For the moment Michelle reconciled herself to putting her career on the back burner. "The way I look at it is, *we're* running for president of the United States. Me, Barack, Sasha, Malia, my mom, my brother, his sisters—we're all running," she says. "I can't hold down a full-time job as vice president of community and external affairs and be on the road three or four days a week."

Michelle made it clear that it was her choice and hers alone. "Barack has never asked me to stop doing my job; as far as he was concerned, 'You have to do whatever makes you feel comfortable.' But, for me, it was: How can I not be part of this? How can I go to work every day, when we're trying to do something I believe in? If I really felt it was more important for me to be vice president of community and external affairs full time, I would do that."

In the end, Michelle said that she sees her situation as nothing less than historic, and she accepts that. "The bigger goal here is to get a good president— somebody I believe in, like Barack, who's really going to be focused on the needs of ordinary people. . . . We have this opportunity, and Barack could do amazing things."

Whenever she was at home during this period, Michelle tried to carry on her life with her children as normally as possible. "Our lives are so close to normal, if there is such a thing when you're running for president," she said. "When I'm off the road, I'm going to Target to get toilet paper, I'm standing on soccer fields, and I think there's just a level of connection that gets lost the further you get into being a candidate."

Although Malia and Sasha knew what their parents were doing, they remained somewhat insulated from much of the turmoil of the campaign. The girls continued to live their active young lives with artistic pursuits such as piano and dance lessons balanced with sports such as tennis, soccer, and gymnastics. Michelle herself tried to work out for ninety minutes three times a week.

When asked if the children were overwhelmed by "the whole thing" by Katie Couric on CBS News, Michelle replied, "They're not because . . . this isn't their life. You know we've done the best that we can to keep them on course. So they're in the same school with the same teachers, with the same friends. And fortunately they go to school where people, you know, they've known us a while."

What kinds of things did the next First Family's kids talk about? "They're talking about Valentine's Day," said their mother, as she listed the ordinary details of a six-year-old's and nine-year-old's lives. "And Sasha finished her cards. She had two left, and she finished them. And they have to take them tomorrow. And one's got a field trip. And they're gonna have pizza for lunch."

Other details concerning the running of the

Obama household were covered by the "Obama House Rules" as listed in the August 8, 2008, issue of *People* magazine:

1) "No whining, arguing or annoying teasing," says Michelle Obama.

2) Make the bed. "Doesn't have to look good—just throw the sheet over it," says Michelle.

3) Set your own alarm clock. "They get themselves up, get their own clothes," says Sasha and Malia's grandmother, Marian Robinson. "They're very easy to take care of. There's not much left for me to do!"

4) Keep the playroom toy closet clean.

5) Allowance from Dad for doing chores: $1 per week. "I'm out of town all the time," says Barack, "so Malia will say, 'Hey, you owe me ten weeks!'"

6) No birthday or Christmas presents from Mom and Dad, who spend "hundreds" on birthday slumber parties and, as Barack puts it, "want to teach some limits." Says Michelle, "Malia says, 'I know there is a Santa because there's no way you'd buy me all that stuff.'"

7) Lights out at 8:30 P.M. "They got an extra half

hour when they were ready to read on their own," says Michelle.

Of course, there were some new visitors to be found at the house those days: a twenty-four-hour detail from the Secret Service. According to *The New York Times*, in May 2007, Michael Chertoff, the homeland security secretary, after conferring with Congress, gave the Obama family this ultimate degree of protection earlier than any presidential candidate in history.

At the time, Michelle told *Newsweek*, "We are grateful the Secret Service is part of it. I'm probably more grateful than Barack, who loves to lead a normal life. This is the first sign that things are not normal." Her girls seem to take them in stride: "They call them the 'secret people,'" said their mother.

While her husband was still working for the Democratic nomination, Michelle Obama began making campaign appearances by herself. This was during the time when Hillary Clinton was still very much a contender for the nomination, and the Obama campaign organization felt that, as a woman, Michelle would be a particularly compelling advocate for her husband's cause.

In a fairly typical appearance, Michelle addressed a crowd in North Carolina in May 2008. Michelle spoke of "just how amazing this journey is . . . a historic journey." In a speech that was representative of the "stump" campaign talk that she gave repeatedly around the country that spring, Michelle went on to speak of her husband's achievements and the great challenges that faced the nation.

Michelle's speech featured many of the points one would expect: Barack Obama's credentials as a legislator, his successes in the campaign to date, and a general outline of what he would accomplish if elected president. Michelle went on to paint Barack as an underdog candidate who refused to crumble in the face of critics. She defended him against those who tried to belittle his achievements.

She went on to give examples regarding his unexpected ability to raise campaign funds, an essential part of any successful race. She talked about Barack's ability to form an effective political organization, and she reminded the crowds of all his wins in tough primary contests. In each case, Michelle pointed out that whenever an obstacle had been overcome, skeptics raised new doubts about his candidacy and his achievements.

In describing these events from the campaign, Michelle was doing more than just revisiting past triumphs to gain more support for Barack. She went further and emotionally linked her audience to the same kinds of hopes and frustrations that they may have encountered in their own lives. "So the bar has been shifting and moving in this race, but the irony is," she said, "the sad irony is that that's exactly what's happening to most Americans in this country. The bar is shifting and moving on people all the time." Michelle showed the crowd that they had a common experience.

Continuing her appeal to the mostly working-class crowd, Michelle added, "And folks are struggling like never before, working harder than ever, believing that their hard work will lead to some reward, some payoff. But what they find is when they get there and the bar has changed, things are different. . . . So you have to work even harder."

During this period, Michelle would typically be away from home two or three days a week, and Barack, too, was away most of the time. This schedule was possible because Michelle was secure in knowing that her children, Malia and Sasha, were safe at home in Chicago. Michelle's mother, Marian

Robinson, was the crucial link in the family chain of command. "Thank God for Grandma!" Michelle has said more than once on the campaign trail. "I am here today because my seventy-year-old mother is at home with my kids."

Jumping off from that very personal reference, Michelle, in typical fashion, then moved on to a more general social observation that is a talking point of the Obama campaign: the need for better day-care facilities. "If you're a working mother out there, there is nothing like Grandma, see, because now that we all have to work . . . and we're living in a society where child care is unaffordable, it's not accessible. So now we've got young mothers, young parents, worrying about their kids as they're off at work."

It was a surprise to no one that the Princeton- and Harvard-trained lawyer and successful business-woman could organize her facts in a campaign speech. Her education and experience gave her those skills. But Michelle's speeches were much more than words on paper. What is exceptional is Michelle's ability to reach out to people of all types and backgrounds. One audience member in Water-loo, Iowa, said, "She's so dynamic, but she speaks from the heart and that's what I'm looking for."

When campaigning, Michelle showed a ready ability to adjust her demeanor depending on the circumstances and makeup of the crowd. Geraldine Brooks, a journalist who covered the Obama campaign, described meeting Michelle on two occasions. The first time was on Martha's Vineyard at an evening fund-raiser. The journalist found her to be "pleasant but detached as she worked the room. I got the impression that she would much rather have been at the beach with her daughters."

The second time was at a campaign event in Montana, one of the last before the Democratic primaries. Here, Brooks said, "Michelle is entirely different. Casually elegant in a silver-gray sweater over linen pants, she moves through the crowd as if she is genuinely enjoying each encounter. Warm, focused, she switches easily from light banter with those who want to just shake her hand to grave attentiveness with those who buttonhole her about policy."

Larry King asked about the impact of race in the campaign in a televised interview with Michelle. She replied that the campaign was less about race than it was about shared values and common hopes.

Referring to her travels on the campaign trail, she said, "The thing that I've always found and what makes me hopeful, especially when I travel around places like Iowa and places where there are not that many black folks, is that where I connect with people is around values. It's around the stories of my upbringing, you know, growing up in a working-class background. . . ."

Michelle went on to say that she can find a way to discuss the issues that goes beyond politics and partisanship. "The notion that you treat people with decency and respect even if you don't always agree with them or don't know them—you know, people hear that. And it reminds them of who they are and who they hope to be. And that transcends race."

In the months of campaigning, with the microscope-like scrutiny that candidates (and their wives) were under, it was inevitable that some of the things Michelle said would be seen in a poor light. Especially early on, when she was less guarded, Michelle's spontaneous nature got her into some hot water.

For instance, when she made a reference to some of Barack's more human faults, like snoring or not putting his socks in the hamper, some critics said she was belittling him. When asked about that controversy in an interview in *Glamour*, she replied, "I think [most] people saw the humor of that. People understood that this is how we all live in our marriages. And Barack is very much human. So let's not deify him, because what we do is we deify, and then we're ready to chop it down. People have notions of what a wife's role should be in this process, and it's been a traditional one of blind adoration. My model is a little different—I think most real marriages are."

Addressing the question of her flippant use of humor more generally, Michelle was quoted in *The New York Times* as saying, "What I've learned is that my humor doesn't translate to print all the time. But usually when I'm speaking to a group, people understand what I'm trying to say, they get the humor, they understand the sarcasm, they get the joke."

There was another occasion when Michelle's words would be misinterpreted, generating a media storm that wouldn't die down for months. Addressing a rally in Wisconsin in January 2007, speaking without a script, Michelle enthused to a cheering crowd, "For the first time in my lifetime, I am really proud of my country, because it feels like hope is finally making a comeback."

The first part of the quote was pounced on by various commentators as evidence of Michelle's (and, by extension, Barack's) lack of patriotism. Cindy McCain, wife of John McCain, then the presumptive Republican nominee for the presidency, was particularly relentless in her attack on the Obamas, stating repeatedly, "I've *always* been proud of my country." It was incidents such as this one that provoked Barack Obama to demand that people "lay off my wife" during an appearance on *Good Morning America.*

David Axelrod, the chief strategist of the Obama campaign team, said this about Michelle's straight-talking style: "Occasionally, it gives campaign people heartburn. She's fundamentally honest—goes out there, speaks her mind, jokes. She doesn't parse her words or select them with an antenna for political correctness."

The road that led to the 2008 Democratic National Convention began back on February 10, 2007, when her husband, Barack Obama, the junior senator from Illinois, declared his candidacy for the office of president of the United States. Michelle Obama stood beside him when he said, "Each and every time, a new generation has risen up and done what's needed to be done. Today we are called once more—and it is time for our generation to answer that call. . . ."

In the months that followed, Michelle Obama would campaign by her husband's side and, if the need arose, on her own. She believed in Barack's aspirations and was ready to help him make his dream become a reality. As she simply stated, "I come here as a wife who loves my husband and believes he will be an extraordinary president."

The night of the convention, Michelle spoke about another role that was a top priority for her: being a mother to her two daughters, Malia, then ten years old, and Sasha, then seven. "I come here as a mom whose girls are the heart of my heart and the center of my world," she said. She added, "They're the first thing I think about when I wake up in the morning, and the last thing I think about when I go to bed at night."

The momentous step that she and her husband were about to take would have much greater significance than the achievement of one man or even one family. The election of a president would have an impact on every person living in the United States. Michelle believed that Barack Obama could make a difference in the lives of all Americans. Michelle made it quite clear why she was supporting her husband in his historic bid. The most important reason came from her experience as a mother. In the "One Nation" speech she gave at the 2008 Democratic National Convention, she said, "Their future—and all our children's future—is my stake in this election."

Throughout her speech Michelle Obama referred to "hope." She explained how her own life story is an example of the dreams and aspirations shared by many Americans. "That is the thread that connects our hearts," she said. "That is the thread that runs through my journey and Barack's journey and so many other improbable journeys that have brought us here tonight." Sounding a theme that would be repeated in the months to follow, Michelle Obama symbolically placed her husband's campaign at a crossroads "where the current of history meets this new tide of hope." She added patriotically, "That is why I love this country."

Michelle Obama talked about her great hope for both her own future and that of her country. Michelle gave credit to her stay-at-home mom and blue-collar dad for the achievements she has made in her life.

"My mother's love has always been a sustaining force for our family." She added, "Dad was our rock . . . he was our provider, our champion, our hero."

She talked about the family as a crucial building block of society. "Barack and I were raised with so many of the same values . . . and [we] set out to build lives guided by these values, and pass them on to the next generation." She stressed how both she and Barack felt that their children's future was the motivation for hope, that "we want our children—and all children in this nation—to know that the only limit to the height of your achievements is the reach of your dreams and your willingness to work for them."

She shared how, on one of their first dates back when both she and her husband-to-be were working for the same law firm in Chicago, Michelle had learned about Barack's work as a community organizer. "You see, instead of going to Wall Street, Barack had gone to work in neighborhoods devastated when steel plants shut down and jobs dried up." Michelle was impressed that Barack chose a career path that could help other people instead of choosing one that would lead only to personal wealth.

Michelle Obama recalled that her husband had taken off his jacket, rolled up his sleeves, "stood up that day, and spoke words that have stayed with me ever since. He talked about 'the world as it is' and 'the world as it should be.' And he said that all too often, we accept the distance between the two, and we settle for the world as it is—even when it doesn't reflect our values and aspirations." She said that the future president then "urged us to believe in ourselves—to find the strength within ourselves to strive for the world as it should be. And isn't that the great American story?"

Michelle Obama's reminiscence was her call to action to an audience she was trying to sway into supporting the inspiring ideals her husband stands for. It is also clear that Barack's ideals had a profound effect on her own life. The career choice she made after meeting Barack—leaving a high-paying job as a corporate lawyer to work in the public sector for the city of Chicago—is one such example.

As she introduced her husband as the Democratic nominee for president, Michelle looked back once again on her own "improbable journey," the path she took to become the woman she is today and the debt that she feels as an American. "And in my own life, in my own small way, I've tried to give back to this country that has given me so much. That's why I left a job at a law firm for a career in public service, working to empower young people to volunteer in their communities. Because I believe that each of us—no matter what our age or background or walk of life—each of us has something to contribute to the life of this nation."

Michelle spoke eloquently of the journey that brought her to this historic occasion. She acknowledged the past that helped form her and inspires her still to strive onward to the next challenge. Introducing her husband, the first African American in history to be successfully nominated for the presidency by a major party, Michelle looked back on their shared history and, most important, *forward* to the next part of the journey that they would begin together.

"So tonight, in honor of my father's memory and my daughters' future—out of gratitude for those whose triumphs we mark this week, and those whose everyday sacrifices have brought us to this moment—let us devote ourselves to finishing their work; let us work together to fulfill their hopes; and let us stand together to elect Barack Obama president of the United States of America."

Michelle Obama learned many hard lessons during the presidential campaign that would see her husband in the White House, but she would emerge with a newfound sense of self-awareness. In October 2008, just before the presidential election, Michelle told an interviewer, "This might be a confusing journey if I were thirty or twenty. But at forty-four, fortunately, I'm more comfortable with who I am and I'm more clear about who I am. Had I done this ten years ago, I don't think I could have done it with as much enjoyment. It would have been more painful. Now all the hard stuff really just rolls off your back."

12 To the White House

Throughout the campaign Michelle Obama was often asked what she would do if she reached the White House. "I've thought about it a lot and I get asked it a lot," she said in an interview. Then, reflecting on her own background and experience, she added, "But there are a lot of things that I care about. I mean, I ran . . . a national service program, so I care deeply about national service. I work for an academic medical center, so I know the challenges in health care."

She has been an advocate for more rights for women. Educating the country's children is a huge priority in her mind. "There are a ton of things. It's endless what you can do in the White House," she said. "But until I get there and know what kind of resources I'll have and how much time and what's the agenda of the country, I think, truthfully, I don't know which of these many things I can focus on."

Michelle has said that she doesn't expect her character or personality to change as a result of her husband being elected president. She prides herself on being true to herself no matter what the situation. When Katie Couric asked her if she was afraid of the "court of public opinion," Michelle replied, "You know, what I vowed is that I want to be as 'me' as I can be so that people, you know, if they vote for Barack, they know exactly who their First Lady will be, all the good and bad. So pretty much what people see . . . is what they get."

Not surprisingly, Michelle's first concern as First Lady will be Malia and Sasha. "What will the girls need?" she asks. "Are they going to transition easily to the White House and this public life and a new school and a new city?"

Summing up, Michelle said, "I think the role of First Lady is a full-time job. And my immediate priority will be to make the White House a home for our daughters. It's going to be a big change for them, and they are going to need my full attention."

As for the girls, Malia and Sasha have their own

priority when they get to the White House—and it has four legs. Since the beginning of the campaign, they have been promised that they can get a dog after the election. In fact, the two already "test-drove" a canine at the White House. They were there on a visit in 2005 and were bored, said their mother, until President Bush's terrier, Barney, showed up. The kids had a great time romping with him on the South Lawn and haven't stopped talking about getting their own dog since.

What lies ahead for Michelle LaVaughn Robinson Obama? Where does her "improbable journey" take her to now? She struggled and strove to rise up from a working-class childhood. She spent years studying at the finest schools her country had to offer. She built a successful career by following her heart and conscience into public service. She met and married an extraordinary man she loved and began raising a family. She worked alongside that man as he made his historic bid for the presidency of the United States. Michelle Obama—"Barack's Rock," as she has been dubbed numerous times in the press—is ready. She's ready to devote her life to her country. She's ready to see her husband inaugurated in Washington, D.C., on January 20, 2009. She's ready to take *her* place in history.

"I think people are ready for something different. But, you know, as I say, I prepare for everything— mentally and emotionally. So I'm ready for the highs, and I'm ready for the lows. But I'm also ready to work with my husband in the White House, as well, and lead this country to a different place."

Glossary

Activist: a person who works to change society

Advocate: a person who speaks on behalf of another

Affirmative action: an effort to provide education and employment opportunities to minority groups, including African Americans, women, etc., through policy and practice

Aide: an assistant, often someone who works for a politician

Alumni: persons who have graduated from a school, or former students of a school

Associate: a junior member in a law firm

AmeriCorps: an organization that sends volunteers all over the United States, particularly to inner cities, in order to teach and work to improve people's lives

Bar examination: a test that determines whether a law

school graduate is qualified to practice law in a particular state

Blue-collar worker: a member of the working class, who performs manual labor and earns an hourly wage

Buttonhole: to delay or prevent

Civil rights: powers that everyone belonging to a society should have. In the United States, civil rights include the right to vote and the right to speak and write freely.

Congress: the branch of the U.S. government that makes the laws for the country. Congress is divided into two groups: the Senate and the House of Representatives.

Conservative: a person who follows a particular set of political views, usually including the belief that government should be involved as little as possible in people's lives and that most problems are better solved by individuals than by the government. In 2008, people tended to think of the Republican Party as the more conservative party.

Consultant: a person who is hired to assist a politician by giving advice and guidance, especially on how to run a campaign

Delegate: a person who votes for a nominee at the national convention of a political party

Diversity: the political and social policy of encouraging tolerance for people of different backgrounds

Epiphany: the sudden realization or comprehension of the essence or meaning of something

Fraternity: an organization formed for any of the following reasons: university education, work skills, ethics, ethnicity, religion, politics, charity, or chivalry, among others

General election: an election between two or more political parties in which the entire population votes for a winner

Georgian architecture: a set of architectural styles popular from 1720 to 1840, characterized by proportion and balance

Gothic architecture: an architecture style of the high and late medieval period. It evolved from Romanesque architecture and was succeeded by Renaissance architecture.

House of Representatives: one of the houses that make up the U.S. Congress. Each state elects representatives (the exact number is based on the state's population) who make laws for the country.

Ivy League: a group of eight private colleges and universities in the northeastern United States. The term is most commonly used to connote academic excellence, selectivity in admissions, and a reputation for social elitism.

Jim Crow: the nickname for a series of state and local laws enacted mostly in the southern United States between 1876 and 1965. These laws segregated African Americans from white Americans in all public facilities and gave them "separate but equal" status.

Keynote speech: an address delivered at a political

convention to set the tone, summarize the primary message of the event, and motivate the attendees

Labor union: a group of workers who band together to bargain with an employer or group of employers

Liberal: a person who follows a particular set of political views, usually including a belief that government should make laws and rules that will solve problems, should protect health and safety, and should make sure all people have the same opportunities. In 2008, people tended to think of the Democratic Party as the more liberal party.

Mentor: a person who provides expertise to a less experienced individual in order to help her advance her career or enhance her education

Partisan: a person who is strongly on one side of an issue. This term is often used to describe someone who is not interested in listening to the other side or willing to compromise.

Partner: a highly ranked position in a law firm, accounting firm, or financial firm

Presumptive: probable or likely

Primary election: an election in which political party members choose the candidate who will represent them in the general election

Progressive: a person who is willing to embrace change or reform

Public service: work that helps society. This term is often used to describe a job in politics.

Seat: the name of the job of a senator. There are 100 seats in the Senate; therefore, there are 100 senators. Each senator has the right to cast a vote for or against a bill.

Segregation: the once-legal public separation of African Americans from white Americans. Segregation was enforced in schools, in restaurants, in restrooms, at drinking fountains, and at movie theaters. Segregation was also used to keep African Americans from moving into white neighborhoods.

Senate: one of the two houses that make up the U.S. Congress. Each state elects two senators, who make laws for the country.

Senator: a person who has a seat in a senate

Talking point: a fact or idea that lends support to an argument

Thesis: a written research paper that is often required for a university degree

About the National Convention

Large national conventions are held every four years by the two major political parties: the Democratic Party and the Republican Party. These gatherings take place in the summer prior to the presidential election, which is held on the first Tuesday of November. Each state's party sends delegates, who represent that state's voters, to vote for the candidate or candidates preferred in their state.

At the conclusion of the convention, each party will have determined who will be its final candidate for president and vice president. During the conventions, each party establishes what is known as a *platform*. It is called a platform because it establishes the ideas and beliefs that the party will support and collectively "stand" on. A party's platform is the road map that the party intends to follow in governing for the next four years.

Some of the issues facing the country today include the status of the economy, health care, the war in Iraq, and many others. National conventions provide a forum for discussion and debate on these issues, to determine what role they will play in the party's platform.

While much of the discussion takes place behind closed doors, the convention culminates in a large hall where speeches are given and the party's chosen candidates are officially proclaimed after a *roll call*, or verbal vote.

Notes

Prologue

1   "Each of us . . .": Obama, Michelle. "One Nation" Speech. Democratic National Convention. Pepsi Center, Denver, CO. 25 August 2008.

Chapter 1, "Hometown: Chicago"

3   "Hog Butcher for the World . . .": Sandburg, Carl. *Chicago Poems*. New York: Henry Holt and Company, 1916.

4   "I am the product . . .": Obama, Michelle. Primary Campaign Stump Speech. Town Hall Meeting. Durham Armory, Durham, NC. 2 May 2008.

Chapter 2, "Growing Up"

8   "Because when you see . . .": Obama, Michelle.

Primary Campaign Stump Speech. Town Hall Meeting. Durham Armory, Durham, NC. 2 May 2008.

8   "... a man who didn't complain ...": Ibid.

8   "That is what gave ...": Ibid.

8–9   "By getting up ...": Ibid.

10   "There was Marian ...": Obama, Barack. *The Audacity of Hope*. New York: Crown, 2006: 330.

11   "We alternated washing ...": Rossi, Rosalind. "The Woman Behind Obama." *The Chicago Sun-Times* 20 January 2007.

12   "This is the person ...": Robinson, Craig. Introductory Speech. Democratic National Convention. Pepsi Center, Denver, CO. 25 August 2008.

12   "It's funny to think ...": Ibid.

13   "I come here as ...": Obama, Michelle. "One Nation" Speech. Democratic National Convention. Pepsi Center, Denver, CO. 25 August 2008.

13   "She set up ...": Rossi, Rosalind. "The Woman Behind Obama." *The Chicago Sun-Times* 20 January 2007.

13   "... let her win enough ...": Ibid.

14   "You never wanted ...": Wolffe, Richard. "Barack's Rock." *Newsweek* 25 February 2008.

14   "We knew you would do this ...": *Harvard Law School Yearbook*. 1988.

15   "And there were uncles ...": Obama, Barack. *The*

Audacity of Hope. New York: Crown, 2006: 330.

15   "When you grow up . . .": Slevin, Peter. "Her Heart's in the Race." *The Washington Post* 28 November 2007.

15   "Our parents gave us . . .": Ibid.

16   "My parents told us . . .": Saulny, Susan. "Michelle Obama Thrives in Campaign Trenches." *The New York Times* 14 February 2008.

Chapter 3, "School Days"

17   "Without being immodest . . .": Rossi, Rosalind. "The Woman Behind Obama." *The Chicago Sun-Times* 20 January 2007.

18   "I don't know . . .": Johnson, Rebecca. "Michelle Obama Interview: 'I'm Nothing Special.'" *Daily Telegraph* 26 July 2008.

18   "More important . . .": Collins, Lauren. "The Other Obama." *The New Yorker* 10 March 2008.

19   "I remember Michelle . . .": Saulny, Susan. "Michelle Obama Thrives in Campaign Trenches." *The New York Times* 14 February 2008.

19–20 "This is not what normal . . .": Rossi, Rosalind. "The Woman Behind Obama." *The Chicago Sun-Times* 20 January 2007.

21   ". . . create a positive . . .": Whitney M. Young Magnet High School website.

22   "When she applied . . .": Mundy, Liza. *Michelle:*

A *Biography.* New York: Simon & Schuster, 2008: 50–51.

22   "It was an industrial . . .": Ibid.

23   "Although it was racially diverse . . .": Ibid. 55.

23   "She was disappointed . . .": Wolffe, Richard. "Barack's Rock." *Newsweek* 25 February 2008.

23   "I'm sure it was . . .": Ibid.

24   "Princeton, the Ivy Leagues . . .": Ibid.

25   "I *knew* him . . .": Ibid.

25   "Michelle works . . .": Johnson, Rebecca. "Michelle Obama Interview: 'I'm Nothing Special.'" *Daily Telegraph* 26 July 2008.

Chapter 4, "Princeton University"

27   "She didn't talk . . .": Wolffe, Richard. "Barack's Rock." *Newsweek* 25 February 2008.

28   "It was, like . . .": Ibid.

29   "I remember being . . .": Johnson, Rebecca. "Michelle Obama Interview: 'I'm Nothing Special.'" *Daily Telegraph* 26 July 2008.

29   "We couldn't afford . . .": Jacobs, Sally. "Learning to Be Michelle Obama." *The Boston Globe* 15 June 2008.

29   ". . . always fashionably dressed . . .": Ibid.

29–30 "The white people . . .": Collins, Lauren. "The Other Obama." *The New Yorker* 10 March 2008.

30   "As more blacks . . .": Robinson, Michelle.

"Princeton-Educated Blacks and the Black Community." Undergraduate Thesis, Princeton University, 1985.

31   "To Mom, Dad, . . .": Ibid.

31   "My experiences at Princeton . . .": Ibid.

Chapter 5, "Harvard Law School"

34   "For example . . .": Robinson, Michelle. "Princeton-Educated Blacks and the Black Community." Undergraduate Thesis, Princeton University, 1985.

34   "Princeton was a real . . .": Jacobs, Sally. "Learning to Be Michelle Obama." *The Boston Globe* 15 June 2008.

34–35 "She has incredible . . .": Rossi, Rosalind. "The Woman Behind Obama." *The Chicago Sun-Times* 20 January 2007.

35–36 "Michelle was a student . . .": Saulny, Susan. "Michelle Obama Thrives in Campaign Trenches." *The New York Times* 14 February 2008.

36   "We got to do . . .": Mundy, Liza. *Michelle: A Biography*. New York: Simon & Schuster, 2008: 84.

36   "She was very mature . . .": Ibid.

37   ". . . it is conceivable . . .": Robinson, Michelle. "Princeton-Educated Blacks and the Black Community." Undergraduate Thesis, Princeton University, 1985.

Chapter 6, "At Law"

41   "It was the most . . .": Mundy, Liza. *Michelle: A Biography*. New York: Simon & Schuster, 2008: 90.

41   ". . . had very little . . .": Ibid. 91.

42   "interesting enough" : Ibid. 92.

42   "She was extremely . . .": Ibid.

Chapter 7, "Meeting Barack"

43   "brilliant . . .": Mendell, David. *Obama: From Promise to Power*. New York: Amistad, 2007: 93.

43–44 "He sounded . . .": Ibid. 93–94.

44   ". . . we had lunch . . .": Ibid. 94.

44   ". . . she knew how to . . .": Obama, Barack. *The Audacity of Hope*. New York: Crown, 2006: 329.

45   ". . . even tried to set . . .": Ibid. 329.

45   "Immediately I liked . . .": Interview with Michelle Obama. CBS *Evening News with Katie Couric*. Broadcast 15 February 2008.

45   "wore her down": Ibid.

46   ". . . to see him transform . . .": Ibid.

46   "People connected with . . .": Ibid.

47–48 ". . . visiting the . . .": Obama, Barack. *The Audacity of Hope*. New York: Crown, 2006: 331.

48   ". . . the kindly, good-humored . . .": Ibid.

48   ". . . pretty and sensible . . .": Ibid.

48   ". . . the hidden toll . . .": Ibid.

49   "For someone like me . . .": Ibid. 331–332.

49   "He didn't talk . . .": Wolffe, Richard. "Barack's Rock." *Newsweek* 25 February 2008.

50   "Barack's game . . .": Mendell, David. *Obama: From Promise to Power*. New York: Amistad, 2007: 100.

Chapter 8, "Michelle Robinson and Barack Obama"

53–54   "I didn't see . . .": Wolffe, Richard. "Barack's Rock." *Newsweek* 25 February 2008.

54–55   "Michelle's head . . .": Obama, Barack. *The Audacity of Hope*. New York: Crown, 2006: 332.

55   "I looked out . . .": Mundy, Liza. *Michelle: A Biography*. New York: Simon & Schuster, 2008: 103.

55   "If I died . . .": Wolffe, Richard. "Barack's Rock." *Newsweek* 25 February 2008.

Chapter 9, "A New Direction"

57   "As far as . . .": Mundy, Liza. *Michelle: A Biography*. New York: Simon & Schuster, 2008: 102.

57–58   "I interviewed . . .": Wolffe, Richard. "Barack's Rock." *Newsweek* 25 February 2008.

59   "She had this . . .": Parsons, Christi, Bruce Japsen, and Bob Secter. "Barack's Rock." *The Chicago Tribune* 22 April 2007.

59   "We would have . . .": Collins, Lauren. "The Other Obama." *The New Yorker* 10 March 2008.

Chapter 10, "Marriage and Family"

62   "Mostly, though . . .": Obama, Barack. *The Audacity of Hope*. New York: Crown, 2006: 338.

62   "There was an . . .": Mundy, Liza. *Michelle: A Biography*. New York: Simon & Schuster, 2008: 115.

62–63 "I'm sure she came . . .": Ibid.

63   ". . . by far the best . . .": Brooks, Geraldine. "Michelle Obama: Camelot 2.0?" *More* October 2008.

64   "Our time together . . .": Obama, Barack. *The Audacity of Hope*. New York: Crown, 2006: 339.

64   "On the nights . . .": Ibid.

64   "As a black kid . . .": Brooks, Geraldine. "Michelle Obama: Camelot 2.0?" *More* October 2008.

65   " . . . highly charged environment . . .": Ibid.

65   "She was great . . .": Ibid.

65   "So calm and so . . .": Obama, Barack. *The Audacity of Hope*. New York: Crown, 2006: 339.

66   "Partly because . . .": Ibid. 338.

66   "My wife's . . .": Ibid. 340.

66–67 "In the end . . .": Ibid. 341.

67   "I cannot be . . .": West, Cassandra. "Her Plan Went Awry, but Michelle Obama Doesn't Mind." *The Chicago Tribune* 1 September 2004.

67–68 "What I notice . . .": Ibid.

68   "People said . . .": Brooks, Geraldine. "Michelle Obama: Camelot 2.0?" *More* October 2008.

68   "I had on . . .": Ibid.

69   "So I built . . .": Ibid.

69   "When you go . . .": Ibid.

69   "She has the ability . . .": West, Cassandra. "Her Plan Went Awry, but Michelle Obama Doesn't Mind." *The Chicago Tribune* 1 September 2004.

71   "How do we . . .": Mundy, Liza. *Michelle: A Biography.* New York: Simon & Schuster, 2008: 170.

71   "My comfort zone . . .": Ibid.

72   "When you're on . . .": Gallegos, Rachel. "Obama's Wife Says U.S. Must Be Ready for Change." *Iowa City Press-Citizen* 21 December 2007.

Chapter 11, "On the Campaign Trail"

73   "The way I look . . .": Bennetts, Leslie. "First Lady in Waiting." *Vanity Fair* website 27 December 2007.

74   "Barack has never . . .": Ibid.

74   "The bigger goal . . .": Ibid.

74   "Our lives . . .": Halloran, Liz. "Q&A: Michelle." *U.S. News & World Report* 1 February 2008.

75   "the whole thing": Ibid.

75   "They're not . . .": Interview with Michelle Obama. *CBS Evening News with Katie Couric.* Broadcast 15 February 2008.

75   "They're talking . . .": Ibid.

76   "Obama House Rules": Sobieraj, Sandra. "The Obamas Get Personal." *People* 8 August 2008.

77   "We are grateful . . .": Wolffe, Richard. "Barack's Rock." *Newsweek* 25 February 2008.

77   "They call them . . .": Lee, Tonya Lewis. "Your Next First Lady?" *Glamour* 3 September 2007.

78   ". . . just how amazing . . .": Obama, Michelle. Primary Campaign Stump Speech. Town Hall Meeting. Durham Armory, Durham, NC. 2 May 2008.

79   "So the bar . . .": Ibid.

79   "And the folks . . .": Ibid.

80   "I am here . . .": Ibid.

80   "If you're a . . .": Ibid.

80–81 "She's so dynamic . . .": Slevin, Peter. "Her Heart's in the Race." *The Washington Post* 28 November 2007.

81   ". . . pleasant but . . .": Brooks, Geraldine. "Michelle Obama: Camelot 2.0?" *More* October 2008.

81   "Michelle is entirely . . .": Ibid.

82   "The thing that I've . . .": Interview with Michelle Obama. CNN *Larry King Live*. Broadcast 11 February 2008.

82   "The notion that . . .": Ibid.

83   "I think . . .": Lee, Tonya Lewis. "Your Next First Lady?" *Glamour* 3 September 2007.

83   "What I've learned . . .": Saulny, Susan. "Michelle Obama Thrives in Campaign Trenches." *The New York Times* 14 February 2008.

83–84 "For the first time . . .": Ibid.

84 "I've *always* been proud of my country . . .": Ibid.

84 "lay off my wife . . .": Ibid.

84 "Occasionally, it gives . . .": Collins, Lauren. "The Other Obama." *The New Yorker* 10 March 2008.

85 "Each and every time . . .": Ibid.

85 "I come here as a wife . . .": Obama, Michelle. "One Nation" Speech. Democratic National Convention. Pepsi Center, Denver, CO. 25 August 2008.

85 "I come here as a mom . . .": Ibid.

86 "Their future . . .": Ibid.

86 "That is the thread . . .": Ibid.

87 "My mother's love . . .": Ibid.

87 "Barack and I . . .": Ibid.

87 "You see . . .": Ibid.

87–88 ". . . stood up that day . . .": Ibid.

88–89 "And in my own life . . .": Ibid.

89 "So tonight . . .": Ibid.

90 "This might be . . .": Brooks, Geraldine. "Michelle Obama: Camelot 2.0?" *More* October 2008.

Chapter 12, "To the White House"

91 "I've thought about it a lot . . .": Interview with Michelle Obama. *CBS Evening News with Katie Couric*. Broadcast 15 February 2008.

91–92 "There are a ton of things . . .": Wolffe, Richard. "Barack's Rock." *Newsweek* 25 February 2008.

92 "court of public opinion": Ibid.

92   "You know, what I vowed . . .": Ibid.

92   "What will the girls need . . .": Ibid.

92   "I think the role of First Lady . . .": Sherwell, Philip. "Michelle Obama: Barack's Powerful Weapon." *Daily Telegraph* 17 February 2008.

94   "I think people are ready for something different.": Interview with Michelle Obama. CNN *Larry King Live*. Broadcast 11 February 2008.